Admonitions
of
Ares

Poetry and Commentary

Dave Muffley

Cover design assistance by Joseph Crance.
Author photograph by Stacie Rosewood-Boyskey

ISBN: 978-1-716-51883-6 (sc)

ISBN: 978-1-7948-0648-1 (e)

Library of Congress Control Number: 2021915814

Acknowledgments

The author gratefully acknowledges the following publications in which some of these poems first appeared:

"Diapasons Beside the Potomac" and "The Admonition of Ares" were selected for Honorable Mention and appeared in the *Heroes' Voices National Veterans Poetry Contest 2017* anthology.

"Nursing" appeared in *Deadly Writers Patrol* magazine, Issue #17, Spring 2020.

Many thanks are owed to my friend and brother-in-arms, Joseph Gary Crance, Major, USAF (ret), novelist, author of the *Ryland Creek Saga.* His encouragement, suggestions, and assistance with editing and artwork were invaluable.

Dedication

The poems in this book are about war—not the glory nor the pity of it, but the crime—armed robbery and murder on a global scale.

Those who participate in war do not gain from it. Those who gain do not participate. The perpetrators of the crime are the profiteers and their puppet politicians, manipulating both sides for their own gain. The victims are the soldiers—of both sides, and also the innocent civilians who just happen to be in the way.

This book is dedicated to all the victims of every war, from before the dawn of our supposed civilization, thru the present, and into the inevitable future.

Those of the past, we can only bless.

Those of the present, we grieve.

Those of the future, we must strive to spare.

Contents

Foreword

For most Americans today, not yet born when it ended or too young to remember it, the Vietnam War belongs to history. In these spare, evocative, and deeply personal poems, Vietnam veteran Dave Muffley brings to that protracted, costly, and divisive conflict the spirit of the World War I poet Wilfred Owen, who haunts these pages.

Like Owen, Muffley bears witness to the horror and absurdity of war. Like Owen, too, in his finest poems, Muffley trusts his imagery to do the work of carrying emotion, with a restraint more powerful for being implicit.

The people who populate this book—Muffley's buddies who survived and the many who did not, an army hospital nurse in the wrong profession, a nursing mother sitting in the squalor of a Saigon alley with her human dignity intact, a Viet Cong soldier whose life the poet hopes he did not end, and many more—are brought to life with cinematic clarity.

Read these poems to have your perspective on the Vietnam War, and all wars, permanently changed.

Catherine Tufariello, poet, author, translator

Preface

I didn't set out to be a poet. I trained to be a musician, studying classical pipe organ and jazz trombone. The poetry just seemed to happen along the way.

The times being what they were, I served with the U.S. Naval Advisory Group in Vietnam as essentially a bodyguard for non-combatants – mostly chaplains but sometimes medical personnel, high ranking officers, and a couple of times, a journalist. It was independent and isolated duty, travelling almost daily to very remote outposts wherever Navy or Marine Corps, and sometimes Army personnel were stationed.

My duties did involve considerable exposure to enemy fire. But there were positive tradeoffs, including, because of the unpredictable travel, being exempt from standing scheduled watches and other regular military duties, as well as enjoying a relaxed level of military discipline.

Although an enlisted man, most of my time was spent in the company of one or more officers. Contrary to naval tradition, they often treated me with the courtesy and respect due a fellow human being, and some even took me into their confidence, sharing thoughts, fears, and philosophies. We spent days travelling together by jeep, truck, boat, or helicopter and passed each night at a different isolated outpost among strangers who became our comrades in arms. We joined them in whatever they were doing and shared in whatever fate befell them.

I often found myself under fire, and at times returning fire alongside men I didn't know, defending positions—both physical and philosophical—which were not my own. This unique duty afforded me a wide-angle view of the conflict that was Vietnam.

The poems and interspersed comments which follow express my emotional responses to what I witnessed there.

Dave Muffley

I. In-country

Opening Salvo

I do not open with what I consider my strongest poem but rather my first ever. I had no inclination toward poetry until I was recalled from the bush for temporary reassignment as a replacement for the loss of someone like myself. I hitched a ride in the back of an Army deuce-and-a-half and stood in the bed of that truck just behind the canvas cab roof.

Watching the countryside pass by, I noticed many of the rice paddies were broken by raised sections set aside as small family cemetery plots. There, the people who had spent their lives working those wet fields were buried above the surface in plastered-over mounds. Seeing the number of them, I wondered how many of those graves had been filled by this war?

As I pondered, the steady drone from the diesel stack and jostling of the truck faded from consciousness, and I seemed to be looking through a dark haze of fog and smoke which gave way to a dim scene of people moving about slowly.

They were soldiers from many different nations, ethnicities, and bygone eras. There were strange interactions, such as a Roman legionnaire and an Iroquois warrior on opposite ends of a stretcher, bearing a contemporary soldier, while a U.S. Civil War confederate and a WWI doughboy silently labored together digging a hole.

While I tried to make sense of the vision, a young officer, hatless and in a soiled uniform of the Napoleonic era, strolled into the foreground of my view. He continued panning left past the others as he spoke directly to me. His words stayed with me until I arrived at the small base of Nha Be and haunt me to this day. There, I wrote down his words under the title, "Memorial to the Misled."

Memorial to the Misled

The soil now damp, and pollen, sweet,
that stirring scent of Spring
suggests another renaissance,
a new awakening.

It's now the hour when birds of song
on every bough appear
to chime the dawning of the day
and sing of life, so dear.

But last night, stench of shot and shell
fire made all else give way,
and only thunderous cannon roar
bid answer to the jay.

The turmoil has since quieted,
survivors need not hurry.
Our task is now to make a grave
for comrades whom we bury.

This hill, for which they fought and died,
with birch and hemlock tree
indeed, will make a worthy scene,
but they will never see.

They cannot feel the cool of night
nor hear the crickets sing,
and never will they offer thanks
for flowers friends may bring.

They cannot harbor thoughts of hope
or noble aspiration
for families, once dear to them
or one external nation.

To state's strong values they offer up
their loyalty no longer.
The value of the lives they lost
was infinitely stronger.

For superficial church or state,
their lives they'd blindly give.
If we could now inquire of them,
perhaps they'd rather—live.

After travelling 70 miles south from Nha Be, I arrived at Logistical Support Base Binh Thuy, out of which I would operate for a while. There, I found some of my predecessor's personal effects that had been left behind. Among those items were a few books of poetry, including works of Robert Frost, Jonathan Swift, and John Donne, who advised to "send not to know for whom the bell tolls."

I knew, it tolled for me.

One night, things went badly at a place called Song Ong Doc. In the morning aftermath back at Binh Thuy, I was shocked and angry. I let those feelings bleed out through a pen.

The numbers in "To the Victor and the Vanquished" are for effect and are not a reflection of that night or any one event.

To the Victor and the Vanquished . . .

With faith that our leaders would never misguide,
we fought for the greater good to reign.
For raining the greater genocide
on our foes, we are heroes throughout our domain.
But thirty-one comrades who fell at our side,
whose lives were spent to purchase that plain
will not share the bounty they sanctified
nor profit from ordinances we ordain.

Our loved ones will see that we're glorified,
except thirty-one sweethearts and wives who remain
unconvinced that our action was justified,
to whom we must somehow try to explain
while forty-three children wait outside
for Daddy to play with them again,
and sixty-two once-proud parents decide
if national pride is now worth the pain.

We'll be praised and paraded, far and wide,
led by scores of generals—pompous and vain,
while five hundred congressmen strut to our stride,
and thousands of bureaucrats sing the refrain.
They all hear the results in the rear and divide
the spoils by our toils and count it as gain
that our triumph was clearly quantified;
we left more than two hundred enemy slain.

Now all those involved are quite satisfied,
except two hundred sweethearts and wives who remain
unconvinced that our action was justified,
to whom we don't even care to explain,
while four hundred, once-proud parents decide
if national pride is now worth the pain,
and six hundred children wait outside
for Daddy to play with them again . . . .

Not every day in Vietnam brought a steady stream of blood, sweat, and tears, though.

There were times we found ourselves drenched by beer, refreshing rain, but tears just the same although for various reasons.

How we reacted to those few moments of relaxation was a personal matter.

The poem that follows reflects my reaction.

R&R

For just a stolen pause,
this perfect evening is my own.
The clinking glass, the giggle
of the bar is far below.
By slinking up a ladder
to the roof, I am alone.
My hired friends and lovers
didn't even see me go.
The blaring of the jukebox
has become a muted tone.
The mourning dove at evening
sings a song I'd rather know.
Above the booze and black light
I have found a twilight zone.
From this small height, I see
reality has much to show.

While down below the room
was thick with clouds of cheap perfume,
and incense fogged my thoughts
as much as whiskey slurred my speech,
up here the air is clear,
and I can smell the orchids bloom
and comprehend the beauty
in the sights my eyes now reach.
The thrills of life are not
the shallow pleasures I consume
For those do not enlarge me,
they have nothing more to teach.
To satisfy my senses
and expand my standing room,
I'll climb the roof and look
beyond the bars of China Beach.

The time I spent in the company of circuit-riding chaplains was destined to be influential. I came to know more than twenty chaplains of every order or denominational persuasion: Jesuit, Baptist, Lutheran, Adventist and others.

Some were truly inspiring. Others were real jerks. All seemed fonder of their differences than their similarities.

I heard many sermons, ranging from responsive rituals through the religious symbolism of Charles Schulz's *Peanuts* cartoons to the social mores in the folk music of Simon & Garfunkel or Peter, Paul & Mary.

Filtering them through the universality and tolerance of the local Buddhists and Cao Dai, I reasoned it all boiled down to Christ's Golden Rule, which could also be stated as the Wiccan Creed: "As long as you harm no one, do as you wish."

I concluded, each tradition has truth, but each is merely a drop in the entire sea of truth. Insisting one's own brand of morality is the one-and-only truth is, ironically, immoral.

Many religious traditions are based on the origin mythology of one, Middle Eastern culture. Many of those myths had been, in turn, adapted from previously recorded legends of Egyptian, Sumerian, and other still earlier cultures.

Only that one tradition, however, had the lasting effect of being spread across the known world by the edge of a Roman sword.

Extrapolating from one well-known example common to many ancient cultures, I wrote the following:

Seven Days of Destruction

And on the seventh day,
while God rested,
man was fruitful and multiplied
and filled the earth to subdue it.

And man saw everything that God
had made and behold, it was not enough.
So, on the eighth day, to fill the void,
man created greed.

To satisfy his greed, man took
that which was his neighbor's
by killing his neighbor.
Thus, on the ninth day,
man created death.

Now to protect himself from the greed
of his neighbors, on the tenth day,
man created cities.
To build cities, man took
the dust of the earth. Man slew
swarms of living creatures,
the vegetation, plants, trees,
the fish of the sea, the birds
that fly above the earth, the beasts
of the field, and everything
that has the breath of life.

To have dominion over the cities,
man created governments.
And governments separated
the rich from the poor.
Governments called the rich—master
and the poor—servant.
And there was evening and morning,
the eleventh day.

Now each servant, master,
city and government
looked upon the other and saw
that the other was not good.
Thus, on the twelfth day,
man created hate.

Hate crept upon the minds of man,
and man saw everything that he
had created and saw that he had power—
power to destroy the neighboring
city or government.
So, on the thirteenth day,
man created war.

And on the fourteenth day,
the earth was without form and void,
and darkness
was upon the face of the deep.

The next two poems express feelings I cannot share verbally, even after more than fifty years. The feelings start in the stomach, catch in the throat, then rise to the level of the eyes and there spill out, rendering me speechless.

I can only convey them to you in poetry.

Red Sky at Night

Red star cluster pop flares pierce the night
to signal someone's in a firefight
and calls for help. But they're too far away
for us to get there quick and join the fray.
All we can do is watch and dread the sight.

But wait, a helo comes to lend a hand.
Its cloudbursts of red death now drench the land
and soak the jungle floor with pools of blood,
turning it to slimy, crimson mud.
It's doubtful any enemy still stand.

With hopes to find all from our side alive,
we close the gap. At daylight we arrive
to find the scene where last night's fight took place
and hopefully return them to our base.
We learn that all but one of ours survive.

Now men from both sides lie among the dead,
and theirs, like ours, were equally misled.
Their only guilt, the country of their birth.
For that, we judge their lives of lesser worth.
But it's their land; the guilt is ours instead.

Red Sky in Morning

I crouched and peered above the sandbag wall,
exposed, despite my fear from a close call.
To see my sights in darkness, I await
a flare to light the night and concentrate
on where that last pink flash was I recall,

align my sights and fire at that place,
then move and watch for flash again, in case
my own flash marks my spot and draws his fire.
From elsewhere, I would watch and reacquire
the target if it makes another trace.

But it did not, and then all shooting stopped.
Secured from general quarters, we soon dropped
our guard, and I went soundly back to sleep,
assured that those who had the watch would keep
me safe till morning light. Too soon, I popped

awake and joined the few who ventured out
beyond our base's perimeter to scout
for further enemy or damage done
in last night's firefight. We found one.
But that he'd do no harm, we had no doubt.

A boy, no more than fourteen, lying there
in such a peaceful pose, without a care
as though asleep, but lifeless on the dirt,
in shorts, sandals, sleeveless undershirt
now pierced by bullets, bloodstained, and threadbare.

I wished that I could lift him up and shake
his body, slap him back awake,
demand to know why he did not lose heart
and just go home before the battle's start,
his being dead now just a big mistake.

But crimson clouds provided ample warning.
This would be a day of guilt—and mourning.

I always tend to seek a higher perspective whenever facing things beyond my own control. I withdraw to view a bigger picture and a longer timeline and find solace in the relative insignificance of unfortunate events.

One occurrence might have struck me as just another day out on circuit, but it seemed to stick in my subconscious.

One day, a lieutenant arrived at Ben Luc with four of his men in two skimmer boats to pick-up supplies. A skimmer boat is a small, 14-foot, blunt bow craft with an engine in the rear, a helm just aft of amidships, and is not unlike a boat one might use for bass fishing, except for an M60 machinegun mounted forward near the bow.

The lieutenant was the senior advisor at Tra Cu, a small Advanced Tactical Support Base (ATSB) upriver, where a dozen or so navy personnel had not had a visit from a chaplain in some time. Reasoning we could make our way from there to the other ATSB's farther upriver at Moc Hoa and Thuy Nhon as transportation might arise, it was decided Ben Luc's chaplain and I would ride along with them back to Tra Cu in the morning.

At dawn, we found that the first boat, loaded with supplies, didn't have room for us, so we joined the lieutenant in the second boat, which left an hour later. After a hurried breakfast and in full morning light, we headed upriver with our gunner at the bow, the chaplain and lieutenant amidships, the coxswain at the helm, and me seated at the stern.

About midway, we encountered a brief but harrowing firefight on the river. Somehow, we suffered no casualties. We got to Tra Cu around noon to learn that the earlier boat had never arrived.

The senior advisor stormed off, the chaplain went quiet, and I sat on a sandbag wall to have a smoke. No one spoke while all hands present shared a pot of chili.

I didn't know the missing men.

I thought I'd made it through unscathed.

But some days later . . .

The Stars Don't Care

I climbed this bluff to steal a moment's peace
and stayed to watch the sun set just for me.
Though not alone, another refugee
from harsh reality now seeks release

as well. Along the inlet's other side,
a woman slowly steps into the flow
reflecting fading sunset afterglow.
She hesitates, unsure the night will hide

her nakedness, then turns and looks around
until she's sure that no one near can see.
Convinced she is alone, she feels free
to raise her robe and place it on the ground.

She wades into the tepid, muddy cove
and settles down, submerged to shoulder deep.
Her chores are done, her children are asleep,
a pot of tea is brewing on the stove

for later. First, she needs to wash away
the soil of daily toil and stain of tears
that start each time her heart is pierced by fears
her absent husband may be in harm's way.

She hugs herself as he would, were he here,
the way he did before they took him far,
against his will, to fight their senseless war.
She seeks relief from loneliness and fear.

I should not stay, but now I cannot rise.
Were I to stir, I'd cause embarrassment.
Though voyeurism isn't my intent,
I feel I must remain and let my eyes

bear witness to her pain. She starts to cry,
then wipes away her tears and lifts her head.
Now leaning back, she floats as on a bed
and stares up toward the first stars in the sky.

She seems to whisper, I suppose a prayer
that he'll come home to her alive and well.
Which side he fights for, I've no way to tell.
It makes no difference; the stars don't care.

Might he have been among the enemy
who fired from cover on the riverside
at the small boat in which I got a ride
upriver? Caught exposed, we tried to flee.

Our machinegun mounted forward could not bear,
so just my rifle firing from the stern
protected us until we reached a turn
in the river. I wonder, was he there?

How effective was my fire? Could it be
that I brought all his efforts to an end?
Or were we saved by just the river's bend?
I pray it also kept him safe—from me.

A good day in Vietnam was when we got mail.

An even better day was when we got a movie, which sometimes came along with the mail delivery. The movies were always three reels in olive drab boxes strapped together.

Sometimes, instead of all three reels of the same movie, there would have been a mix-up resulting in our receiving two reels of a spy flick then the middle reel of a western, or some such combination.

We would enjoy it anyway.

Metamorphosis

As a teen in the drive-in movie days,
I attended devoutly every Friday night
and worshiped the stars and the scripts
from the front seat of my car.

As a young man in the military,
an exile from the world, I saw
every movie that came to my firebase,
my only references to reality.

I rolled down my sleeves
and turned up my collar
against the mosquitoes,
found a seat on a log,
and cooked beans over a Sterno fire.

As I rested my rifle against my knees
and stirred my beans in the blue flames,
I heard the rapid-fire crackling
of the projector spitting light
at a sheet of canvas
nailed to a wooden crossbeam.

I alternately scanned the screen,
the slowly simmering beans,
and the ominously open sky,
wary of fatal falling stars
directed at my comrades and myself
exposed in the clearing
at a predictable place and time.

Some movies made me laugh,
many made me cry,
a few disturbed me deeply,
but one changed me forever.

On a sticky Mekong Delta night,
I saw *The Last Valley*.
Set during the Renaissance,
it gathered together
the guardians of truth
and set them at each other's throats.

The soldier, the scholar,
the politician and the priest
all competed to control
the last untouched valley and village
which, were it not for them,
might have remained at peace
amidst thirty years of war.

In that war, Catholics and Protestants,
each with God on their side,
laid all of Europe in rubble
and half its population in graves
fighting over their interpretations
of Christ's Golden Rule.

In the movie's final scenes,
the soldier lay dying
in the arms of the scholar.
With his last breath, I heard him say,
"If you ever find God,
tell him—we—created . . ."
He died without finishing the thought.

I could not decide if the author meant
we created God,
or we created death.
Either seemed equally true.

Still undecided, I climbed into my bunk
and pulled shut the mosquito net.
Inside that cocoon, I felt
the first stirrings of a metamorphosis—
A soldier lay dying
in the arms of a scholar.

After my first two years in-country, in the spring of 1972, I found myself at Tan Son Nhut Air Base in Saigon, about 100 miles from where I had been in my last freeze frame of consciousness.

To this day, I've no idea how I came to be there, nor how much time had lapsed between the two scenes, except that it was dark in one and then daylight in the next.

Recognizing my surroundings, I looked up an acquaintance. After learning that my last known location had been given up, I arranged a new assignment for myself. I also discovered I needed medical care.

The following poem tells its own story.

Nursing

She took the blood from my arm
without seeing my face
and handled the tubes with expert care
not to spill a drop on her immaculate
uniform, starched and stretched
to display what it concealed.

Without speaking a word,
she thrust her hand toward me
holding a specimen jar,
with one manicured finger
pointing toward a door
and turned her head away.

I watched her for days
and observed that she spoke
only to doctors. To them she looked up
and smiled, batting her lashes
and bouncing her pert little
hairdo.

She knew that the men in the ward
all watched her. The sound of her steps
made them pull against their pain
to watch her walk by and sigh
at the only "round-eye"
they'd seen in months.

She'd lower her stare
and lift her nose,
pull back her shoulders
and tighten her buttocks,
walking a bit faster past
the sight and smell of their wounds.

The morning she checked me out
of Third Field Hospital
I felt a shudder of relief
to be leaving her care.
I walked to the street and turned
without looking back.

I passed through Saigon's hidden alleys,
clogged with children and dogs and dirt.
The alleys clamored with the sounds
of vendors selling monkey meat,
pedicab drivers selling rides
and girls selling their souls.

At a twist in an alley
along the edge of despair
I caught a glimpse of a woman
sitting in the squalor of life,
suckling an infant and a piglet
side by side.

She was middle aged, I'd say by the lines
of her eyes, which bored directly into mine.
She wore the faded and thin
pajamas of a peasant, hanging
loosely around her sagging body, open
to the waist.

In that one glance, I felt her judge me
worthy to know her life, how the war
had carried her husband far from her
and had taken her sons, all trickled away,
and her daughters too, in a sense, each
matriculated into the filth of the alleys.

Her eyes told me how without hesitation,
she sacrificed her own dignity to feed
her child, how all she had left to cling to
was this last son at her breast
and this beast to nourish him
when she no longer could.

Not wishing to intrude, I angled off
but short of the next bend I felt compelled
to turn and reengage her steady gaze.
With renewed faith in human decency,
I nodded my acknowledgement
then walked on.

For this next poem, it's helpful to know that the title, "Hoa" (pronounced, "wah"), means a flower and is often a feminine given name.

Also, just as most cultures have their own origin myths, among those of the Vietnamese, there is a story of their being the issuing offspring from a sexual union between a dragon and a goddess.

Regret can grow from what one does, or from what one fails to do. Similarly, one can mourn the loss of what was or might have been.

And sometimes, the circumstances of our lives are beyond our control.

Hoa

The shaded and shimmering glow from a porcelain lamp
dispersed slowly, enticingly off of black satin and lace
to reveal the evocative silk of her breast and a face
filled with want. The perfume and monsoon made her
 scent sweet and damp.
Her smile hid her tears for my very last night at that camp
before leaving forever. She promised our next life will place
us together, then lowered herself onto me. When our pace
reached its apex, she whispered her wish as she tightened
 her clamp.

The next day and the rest of this lifetime has taken me far
from that dragon's and goddess' daughter who soothed
 my soul's pain
as she gave me some peace in this lifetime, so ravished by
 war,
that small room with the porcelain lamp and monsoon
 driven rain.
I hope that she got what she whispered she wanted from
 me,
and I pray that the promise she made will one day come to
 be.

II. Back in the World

As with most youths, there were many other misadventures. Some were marked with poems, and some passed unmarked.

The more I saw of warfare, the more my outrage at the absurdity of war—the futile sacrifice of the greater to the lesser. If I could not somehow make it stop, I wanted at least to see this war end. I volunteered to extend for three more tours of combat duty and even reenlisted while in-country.

I suppose I needed some sense of closure, which wasn't to be had, then or since. Rather, I stayed and witnessed the last desperate days of the withdrawal of American forces from Vietnam.

Back in the world at my next duty station, I stoically carried on and had an enviable military career going until personal family circumstances compelled me to reluctantly give it up.

In time, I learned life would present other challenges as well.

Soldier's Heart
(Post-Traumatic Stress Disorder)

There is no courage without fear,
        no triumph without test.
To face defeat 'though flight is near
        pays honor to the quest.
To suffer all you see and hear
        yet fight on to your best,
To shield from blows judged most severe
        then stiffly feel the rest,
'Twill spare the body for a year
        but heart and mind infest.
The heart grows numb to what was dear,
        the mind is drained of zest.
Though body heals, the soul will sear
        till nurtured in the nest.
Through venting guilt and shedding tear,
        the hero will be blest.

After giving up my military career, I found my accustomed standards of honor, discipline, and performance were not in line with the civilian workplaces I experienced. I expected much of myself and everyone else.

While I did excel and advance in various endeavors, I also tended to burn out and felt dissatisfied everywhere I went.

I readily admit to some difficulty subordinating myself to seniors whom I did not consider my superiors. But I also felt unaccomplished, even disadvantaged to some extent, by my lack of a credible academic degree.

It's easy to think of ourselves as victims of circumstance. Then it occurred to me that all of us may be, rather, victims of consequence.

Throughout our lives, we make choices, each of which channels our remaining available options. It is for us to weigh our options, make our choice, and accept the outcome. Sometimes, our options are limited beyond our control. Inevitably, we suffer some losses with damage done and lasting effects.

I suppose what's left is how we cope with the outcome.

KIA

I am alive but do not truly live.
The future that I might have known was killed
and buried long ago. The grave was filled
before I even knew. Fate did not give
me time to grieve the loss. I never heard
how I could earn a chance at sweet success,
at least, perhaps, to feel some happiness,
had not my spirit been so soon interred.

So now I persevere but feel despair
at all I might have done but failed to do.
Instead of college, I went over there
and lost life's future growth by twenty-two.
Was it indeed by fate's hand that it died?
Or was it, rather, ruled a suicide?

Through a friend of a friend, I became introduced to a noted bibliographer of English literature with a special interest in the poetry of war. He read some of my work and commented that it was critically comparable to that of Ambrose Bierce and Wilfred Owen. At the time, I had never heard of either of those names. He further suggested I get myself into a classroom.

Through provisions of the Dept. of Veterans Affairs Disabled Veterans Rehabilitation Program, I attended Mansfield University in rural northern Pennsylvania as a middle-aged, non-traditional student and would later graduate with a Bachelor of Arts degree in Mass Communication/Journalism.

Along the way, I managed to learn a few things about poetic devices: rhyme, meter, metaphor, alliteration, repetition, lists, and such.

I remember one homework assignment to write a poem taking inspiration from a photograph. My response was my explanation for not doing so.

Rather, I wrote “No Photos, Please.”

No Photos, Please

I don't need photographs to remind me
of my past, the things I've seen;
I have perfect mental pictures
that never wane.

I used to take photos of places I've
been, but in my nightmares,
I am there still and see
it all again.

Through a lens, reality can be softened out
of focus, filtered to remove the
glare or confined within
a focal plane.

A camera only keeps the sight; it cannot
make one hear the screams, or
smell the burning flesh,
or feel the pain.

I lost my camera years ago and seldom
look at photos; there is no need.
The images stay clear
inside my brain.

nother assignment was to write a letter we would never send. I send it now.

Dave Muffley

Dear Billy

I know I should have written sooner,
but I think of you often, every day.
And I've written about you in my poems.
I couldn't think about you at all
the first years after I saw you last.
But I am better now—or worse.

I went to visit you last June.
I stood at the wall and looked for you,
but I couldn't find you then.
Boswell was there and Wilson, Goldy
and a lot of other guys.
I wish I could have talked to you
then, but I couldn't. We've got a lot
of catching up to do now.

I never told you I got married
and raised two kids, as best I could.
They're twenty and nineteen years now,
and both are gone away to college.
But, just like me, they never write.

You might know their mother. She
was twenty-eight when we saw her
for the last time. I'm forty-one now.
I guess that you're still twenty-five.
You don't know what you are missing.

I haven't laughed much since those days,
not like you used to make me laugh,
but since then, I have cried a lot.
Do you remember how we didn't
know what we would do for a living
when we'd get out and back to the world?

In all these years, I still don't know.
I've had at least a dozen jobs
in half a dozen career fields
and climbed the ranks in each of them,
but never really made a living.

Would you believe I went to college?
I may not be a great deal smarter,
but I have become a little wiser.
My professors went to the State U
to learn about the facts of life
when you and I went to the U-Minh
and learned instead the facts of death.
Which is the higher education?
Can you tell me? You should know;
you earned the terminal degree.

I wonder what you're doing now.
Are you having a good time,
wherever you are? Or are you still
there, wading through the mud and jungle?
I've waded through as dense quagmires
of corruption and incompetence
dealing with bureaucrats and bosses.
The things we did together there
seemed to really matter. We knew
what to do and how to do it,

and we believed we knew the reasons.
It's been my experience since then
that no one truly knows what they're doing
and everyone seems afraid to admit it.
If they ever learned the truth behind it,
they couldn't do it anymore.

Where you are, we trusted only our
abilities and earned our merit.
Here, it seems merit has no meaning.
Most don't strive to do the best they can;
they strain to do the least they must
and feel no shame or pride—or guilt.

Billy, I've got a confession to make:
for years, I didn't write to you
because I felt guilty. I thought somehow
I should have been there right beside you.
I might have helped to clear the way.
Now I've come to understand
there's nothing more I could have done,
and there's no need to feel so bad.

Still, I think of you every time
being here doesn't seem worth it.
A lot of times I wanted to write
but just couldn't do it. I wanted to
send a post card or just a note.
I'd write, "Not having a great time,
thinking of you—wish you were here.
Sometimes, I rather wish I were there."

Well, I've got to be moving on.
You take care. Watch your step!
I'll be seeing you,
Dave

I also had a more challenging assignment to write a villanelle, which requires not only an exacting rhyme scheme and line arrangement, but also repeating the first and third lines from the first stanza at precise placements in the other five stanzas.

I was experiencing a sort of personal problem, more frequent in those days than lately, and I chose to address it in this assignment.

I wanted to make the required repetitions variations on a theme, building in intensity toward a climax and then falling off.

Villanelle for Unwritten Poems

I'm bothered by the poems I must write.
The visions tear my eyes and cloud my mind.
I shake them from my head to sleep each night.

Each morning, they return to block the light,
obstruct my way. I plan my day but find
I'm followed by the poems I must write.

I've tried to turn and face the dreadful fright
but fear the words that lurk will strike me blind.
I shake them from my head to save my sight.

I know I must surrender to my plight
and pen the painful lines I am assigned.
I'm troubled by the poems I must write,

oppressed by powers far too large to fight.
They wrestle with my thoughts—my dreams they bind.
I shake them from my head and lurch upright.

Now soaked with sweat, eyes wide, teeth clenched, fists tight,
the bedsheets holding both my arms confined,
I'm tortured by the poems I must write,
but shake them from my head again tonight.

Some of the most inspirational moments on campus were not in the classroom.

Frequently, they would occur in the quiet moments *between* classes. Sometimes, they'd strike out of the sub-conscious unexpectedly, like a punch in the gut.

But there were also the small pains that came as regular as clockwork.

Wilson's Ring

I didn't know Wilson very well,
didn't even know his given name.
He was just a Huey pilot,
an army warrant officer
Julian, Goldy, and I sometimes flew with
on Dustoff missions just to break
the monotony when things were slow
in our Navy compound on the base.

It's odd that even decades later,
at a college campus on the opposite
side of the world, it is Wilson
who haunts me daily, every hour.

When I heard about Wilson's death,
I had just returned to Binh Thuy
from two weeks travelling in the bush,
escorting a circuit-riding chaplain
to every Advanced Tactical Support Base
in the western half of the Mekong Delta.

I dropped my web gear in my hootch,
grabbed a shower and fresh cammies,
then sat down on my bunk to read
a little poetry from John Donne
before going to the wooden shack
we made into a little club,
to readjust my mind with screwdrivers
and heart wrenching tunes from the tape deck.

My friend, Julian, was already there.
I asked him if anything had happened
while I was in the bush. He said,
"Wilson got shot down, he took
a B40. The whole crew was lost."

I slugged down my first screwdriver,
ordered up two more and asked,
"Will there be a movie tonight?"
Julian answered, "There will,
one came with the mail. Want to go?"
I responded, "Affirmative,"
then threw back my second glass and let
the ice cubes hit me in the teeth.

Julian ordered another round,
while I reloaded my hand, leaned back,
and mostly to myself I said,
"Wow – Wilson! We just flew with him
right before I went out on circuit."
As our local-national barmaid
placed two more within my reach,
I remembered that last flight with Wilson:

We are 40 klicks south of Binh Thuy,
skimming the delta at 90 knots.
The steady thumping of the rotor
wing fades from my consciousness.
The helo seems suspended there,
still and silent, two hundred feet
above the checkerboard rice patties.
It's a balmy dusk in the dry season.
Even from my vantage point,
the sun's pallet of apricot, salmon,
turquoise and rose dims to gray.

On the ground below, an old man walks
a dike from one thatched hut toward another
across the patties. I know his age
by his walk, late 70s I'd say.
I imagine him on his nightly stroll
to join his life-long friend and neighbor
for cheerful chat and a cup of tea.

If his friend is prosperous for a peasant,
there might be a portable black-and-white TV.
The old men can watch costumed actors
with thick makeup enact ancient operas,
dancing beneath their swirling swords,
the twanging of stringed instruments
and flutes accented by cymbals and drums.

The opera vanishes when through the headset
inside my flight helmet, I hear Goldy
at the M60, ask Wilson if we'll
get back to Binh Thuy in time for drinks
at the club. Wilson doesn't answer
into his flight helmet's lip mike,
but turns his head over his right shoulder
and flashes a solid "affirmative"
with his eyes and his handle-bar moustache.

Wilson's right hand is also swung
around to signal a "thumbs up".
I notice a lump beneath his flight glove
and remember it to be a class ring,
gold with a facetted red stone.

For some reason it reminds me
of the pitch a jewelry salesman gave
to the senior class at my high school
a few years earlier. "A class ring
is a symbol of belonging," he'd said.
"It stands for friendship, devotion and loyalty
for many years after you leave this place,
no matter where you go in life."

I glance toward Wilson's other gloved hand
still on the helicopter's joystick.
There I see a smaller bulge.
That other ring, too, is a symbol of belonging.
The memory of that last flight crashed
when Julian advised me to drink up,
the movie would be starting soon.

After the movie, we went back
to the club in time for last call and
the nightly ceremony of the peace bell.
Each night after everyone present
ordered their last drink of the night,
the bar maid would remove the heavy,
brass ship's bell from its stand on the bar,
turn it upside down and pass it around
for everyone to poor their last drink in.

Then, we would pass it around again,
each man drinking from the rim of the bell
until it was empty. We'd ring the bell,
for peace, return it to its stand
then close and secure the club for the night.

That night, I ordered two last drinks,
one for me, and one for Wilson.
I took the bell from the stand myself,
and after we all filled it, I offered it
to each man in turn, like a priest with a chalice.
When it was empty, I ran from the club
and around the base ringing the peace bell
as loud and long as I could, until
I was too tired or too drunk to continue.

Then, I took it back to the club,
restored the bell to its stand on the bar
and stood there alone, listening
to the last waves of its fading tone.

I don't know why Wilson affected me so.
I lost closer friends, including Goldy.
I'll never forget the memorial service
we held when Goldy's crew was shot down:

"It is eight bells, Sir. Our shipmates' watch is done."
"Make it so!"
Ding Ding—Ding Ding—Ding Ding—Ding Ding—
"Bugler—Sound Off!"

That's why whenever I hear *Taps*,
it causes me to think of Goldy.
It was the last thing that I heard.
But it is Wilson for whom the bell tolls.
Every hour, when the campus carillon chimes,
I stop and listen—because the last ring
is for Wilson.

In 1991, three events converged to produce this next poem: I passed much of a night talking with another disabled veteran. I had just finished reading Allen Ginsburg's classic poem, "Howl." And I received a phone call informing me of the death of a close friend.

The next morning, I lie on my bedroom floor with a lined legal pad and a pencil, and paraphrasing the first two lines of "Howl," I wrote:

Cry
(For Tom)

I saw the best minds of my generation
destroyed by America's madness.
They were young, eager, and intelligent.
They wanted to explore the universe,
find a peaceful planet to live on
and smile at its wonders.
They wanted to find a home
where they could draw their share of life
from Buddha's bowl, then pass the bowl
to another happy generation.

But they got lost, each one, along the way.
The loss of those diminished me,
and I am left to explore the universe alone.
Each time one of those young minds vanished,
it was as though a part of me broke away
and drifted off into weightless space with it.

Billy was the first to go.
He was my smile.
He made me laugh so hard my face would hurt.
Billy's mind left him quickly
in a sudden explosion.
My smile flew off with it.

Maggot went the same way, in a burst of mud.
He had taught me to listen
to the small sounds in the night air.
I didn't care if I heard those sounds anymore,
so, I let him take my ears.

Goldy had a quick wit.
His thoughts would fly ahead of our discussions
and add dimensions to our words
His body couldn't fly without machinery
and he fell from the sky in his damaged machine.
His wit got broken in the fall.
I buried mine with him

Wilson's machine didn't fall,
it exploded in mid-air.
The only loyalty I ever felt
was borrowed from Wilson.
I paid it back to his memory when he vanished.

Bubba's mind didn't really go away,
it just didn't work anymore.
We sent him to a hospital to have it fixed,
but some of the parts were bent beyond repair.
One of the parts that got bent was his courage,
and he needed some in that place.
I gave him some of mine.

We didn't know whether Smitty's mind
could be fixed or not,
he couldn't speak.
The words were stuck in his throat.
So, here are some words for Smitty.

Julio's mind leaked out
through a hole in his leg.
It takes longer that way,
long enough for the mind
to know where it's going.
Julian and I loaned him our legs
for about half a click,
but Julio's mind left us
somewhere along the way.

Julian left a few months later.
He just went away one day
without saying where he was going.
Julian was defiant like that,
completely lacking in tolerance.
I'd package all the tolerance I have
and mail it to him,
but I don't know where to send it.

Even Doc doesn't know where Julian went,
and they were close friends.
Doc made fun of Julian's defiance.
Julian defied Doc's humor.
Doc bandaged our wounds with his jokes.
He tried to heal all the wounds in the world
but there wasn't enough humor to go around,
and there were far too many wounds,
so, Doc quit practicing medicine
and raises pigs.
I asked him to tell me why.
He just said, "It's a twisted tale."

Bo doesn't raise pigs on his farm.
He only grows grass.
He says he doesn't like smoking pork
as much as he likes smoking grass.
Bo is hiding behind his smoke screen,
invisible to the naked eye.

Sometimes he loses his naked eye.
He takes it out at night
and can't see to find it in the morning.
We sat and talked one night.
Bo said he had half a mind
to show his half a face
in Washington.
I offered him half of my mind
to take with him.
But Bo said he'd probably lose it
in the grass on the Mall.

Besides, they'd never let him in
to see anyone, and no one
wants to see him, or any of us.
There's a wall there to keep us out.
A lot of us wanted to find homes in America,
but all we got was one wall.
America didn't build it;
America made us build it.
We had to build our own goddamned wall
to keep us out of sight.

A lot of us are there now,
some of the best minds of my generation
invisible behind the smoke
from their trash fire on the Mall,
leaning on crutches and sitting on skateboards,
representing nearly half
of all the homeless in America,
right on America's front lawn,
but America doesn't see them.

Ron is homeless.
I tried to give him my home,
but he didn't know how to use it.
He says he'll know how when he finds his own,
but he can't find it in America.
He's not allowed to hunt for it
without a hunting license,
and he's got to have a home
to get a license.

Don had a license once –
a license to live in peace
together with someone.
But Don couldn't find any peace,
so, the someone with whom he lived
revoked his license.
He can't use mine,
mine expired—years ago.

Denny never tried to live with anyone,
he tried to die by himself.
America gave him a home.
America even built a wall to keep him in.
As far as I know, he's still there
behind the wall for life.
The last time I saw Denny he was crying.
He cried until his eyes ran dry.
I left him all the tears I had.

Maybe that's why now
I don't have any tears left for Tom
Tom might have been the best mind of us all.
He had everything:
a home, a license to live with someone
and another happy generation.

Tom always had a smile.
He was a loyal friend with a good ear
when I needed someone to listen.
His quick wit and humor
were always there to comfort me.
He could see when I was hurting
and he even tried to offer me some smoke
to ease the pain.

Yet my pain was nothing
compared to Tom's.
His youthful face was dioxin scarred on the outside,
like his liver on the inside.
America had sent an agent named Orange
to build a wall inside Tom's body.

It was the only wall America offered him.
Tom didn't want a wall of any kind.
He wanted a new liver,
but America said he had to wait.
Tom tolerated courageously
and waited as long as he could.

Yesterday, I was told Tom's heart stopped working.
He's going to need a new heart
when he finally finds a peaceful
planet to live on.
As Tom flies off to explore the universe alone,
I send him off with these words—
and my heart.

As my college honors project, I worked on a video dramatization of six poems.

One afternoon, I searched diligently in the campus music library for a piece of music I wanted to run with my closing credits. When I was unable to find it, Diane, now my wife, was moved to help by cracking open the music catalog—a fine-printed index about four inches thick—and blindly stabbed her finger down onto a page, saying, "Here! This is the music you are to use for the closing credits."

Haphazard as that may seem, I had already learned not to doubt Diane's gift of guidance. In poetry, sometimes things happen that cannot be explained by any mathematical model. So, I asked to check out the music to which she had pointed. It was Benjamin Brittan's *Requiem*, the composer's symphonic interpretations of the poetry of Wilfred Owen.

There was that name again! Owen was a poet then unfamiliar to me, and with whom it was suggested my work was comparable. I opened the jacket containing several record albums, and there on the inside of the jacket, I found what appeared to be a photograph of my late best friend but in a different uniform.

In shock, I sobbed embarrassingly right there in the library. I listened to the music, agreed it was perfect, and then checked out Jon Stallworthy's edited poetry collection and biography of Wilfred Owen, which bore that same photo on its cover.

A few days later, I attended a workshop conducted by visiting poet, Dr. Linnea Johnson. Concluding with a half hour remaining, she asked the nine of us present to each suggest a topic for a free-writing exercise in the remaining time. She started us off by stating that her own topic would be "things lost, things kept." Around the table, each offered a topic, ending with me.

My proposal was "the impact of an old photograph."

Dr. Johnson suggested I should try combining my topic with hers. My professor, also present, interjected that if I must use rhyme, I shouldn't make it obvious. I wondered how one might make rhyme not obvious and thought, perhaps, to scatter them about at places other than line endings?

After twenty-five minutes of free-writing, I had penned "Things Lost, Things Kept, and a Photo of Billy."

Things Lost, Things Kept, and a Photo of Billy

I lost my ignorance and dread
in blinding light and flame
and crept ahead into the fight,
left shame and innocence
behind me in the night. I kept
a charge that passed to me:
the touch of fear, the sight of hell
the sound of burning huts
and bursting mud, the smell of ruptured
guts, the taste of blood.

I lost my best friend, Billy Owen,
whom I did not know
had left his cold and hallowed trench
to parry at my side
through jungle heat and stench. He taught
me how to stay alive
and how to truly live—then died.
I kept his memory
and wished that I'd had words to give
him in exchange—or cried.

I lost a quarter century
in stoic grief and blame
before I learned that he had slept
for twice that time then rose
and came to me; I saw his face
in a book of poetry.
The oblique pose, sad eyes, thin smile
and mustache were the same,
the uniform style and caption strange:
"Wilfred Owen, 1893-1918"

I lost control and cried at last
and finally understood
that nothing past I'd failed to do
could then have changed his fate.
The wrongful waste, the piteous price
of war again erased
the words that he had not yet said.
His voice was twice, or more
perhaps in other times and fields
struck dead at twenty-five.

I let him sleep in peace again
but strive my best to keep
his words alive. I weep the tears
he would have wept if he
had lived these years. I feel I must,
as though I have no choice.
It is a trust. Strange though it seems,
the friend I knew as Billy
gave me life, but Wilfred kept
as fair exchange—my voice.

It was mid-morning on the third Friday in September, 1996, when I received a phone call from an acquaintance. He informed me of the proclamation that every third Friday in September was to be designated as POA/MIA Recognition Day.

To mark the occasion, there would be a ceremony and enactment on the Green in Wellsboro, Pennsylvania, that evening which would be broadcast live. He asked me to be one of the speakers, representing the veterans who did return home from the war, and how we as a group feel about the POW/MIA issue.

I had recently heard a report by investigative journalists suggesting the U.S. government was aware of POWs still in Vietnam and was even quietly engaged in helping to sponsor them there to counter foreign pressure.

While eating lunch at my desk and drawing from the highlights of news on the radio, I wrote something to present that evening. I could only offer what I personally felt about the POW issue, which for me was a sensitive one.

That evening, wearing a flight suit, with my hands laced together on my head, I and several others were poked and prodded at bayonet point down Wellsboro's Main Street by other vets costumed as Viet Cong, to the Green in the center of town, where we were each placed in individual cages made from bamboo and barbed wire. In turn, we were released from our cages to stand at a lectern and say our piece.

I was the last speaker.

I addressed the crowd by reciting the following:

POW/MIA

I have to believe I saw them fall,
convince myself I'd watched them all,
die valiantly while standing tall,
not huddled in horror behind some wall.

I try to believe I watched as they made
one massive, tragic escapade
four times the size of the Light Brigade,
as daring but doomed as John Brown's raid.

I think of them as hopelessly spent
defending a nation in peril which sent
them there, and they willingly went
without pause to protest, regret, or resent.

That this nation denies them, brings disbelief,
the same nation that pardoned their commander-in-chief
who lied when he said he wasn't a thief,
put thousands of boatpeople on relief

and welcomed deserters in Canada back?
If this government feels that there's too much flack
to bring home its heroes, then our leaders lack
courage and strength, and there must be a crack

in the Liberty Bell. But that cannot be—
not the home of the brave and land of the free.
That might happen in some heartless monarchy
or dictatorship, but not a democracy

where decisions are shared by everyone,
and the will of a well-informed mass is done.
"Withdrawal with honor" didn't mean—overrun
without rescue, and chances of slim—or none.

Our elected leaders would never dare
condemn the righteous to an endless nightmare
while debating the hidden profits in healthcare,
how long should able-bodied get welfare,

how many American goods we can sell
in Ho Chi Minh City but not make them tell
how many Americans still suffer in hell.
No! There are none! They all fell.

Recently, I experienced what it feels like to be the old man at home, watching the news and being powerless to do anything about it, while my own son and my younger stepson were deployed in harm's way.

My son was then an infantry officer, commanding a Stryker company at Tikrit, Iraq. When he returned from his third tour overseas, he was hardly more than off the bus from the airport before being told when he was to take his company back for yet another deployment in Iraq.

His words were, "I am *not* going back *there* again!"

After thirteen years, he resigned his commission and is now a Foreign Service Officer in the State Department diplomatic corps. When between assignments overseas, he spends time in Arlington, Virginia.

A few years ago, my older stepson and I helped him move into an apartment there. I found the Arlington area to be filled with stirring, monumental scenes.

The next poem is my personal anthem to diplomacy. I hoped to use its rhythm and pacing to convey the sounds and thereby also create the image of a somber setting.

Diapasons Beside the Potomac

Row on row of ranks and files,
still standing there prepared to serve
but now serve only dissonance.
Just a fancy, false façade,
the show pipes of a mighty organ,
impotent and tacit now,
they mask the truth that lay beneath
in dust filled chambers where the great
chests swell with wind and sound no longer.
Each pipe used to hold a voice
unique unto itself but now
lies silent in the uniform
constriction of the molded mass.

Closed diapasons—stopped flutes.
Muffled drums—suppressed muzzles.
Muted bugles—stifled cries.

Echoed Taps of time and time
again, still ticking resolute
with practiced metronome precision,
marking not our progress but
our many, frequent, failed attempts
to find accord and harmony
and finally compose a peace,
a perfect melody of man.

As an old man, I'm no longer fit to be a warrior.

I'm not even sure I can pull off being a warrior poet. Perhaps, all I really am, is another disgruntled veteran. Sometimes, it seems that a veteran may be just a soldier who outlived their usefulness to society.

Each Veterans Day, we're misperceived by some to be heroes. When confronted with the supposition, I sometimes reply, "There's no such thing as heroes. There's just survivors."

It's true that at times in our lives, we are faced with difficulties, and we try our best to do what we think is right and necessary, given the situation as we perceive it.

Sometimes it works, and we are praised for it.

But why would anyone ever do otherwise?

In retrospect, we second guess ourselves and wish we could have done more.

The Old Deer

Tonight, from dusk till dark, an old deer stood
and watched, beyond the pond where field meets wood,
as though he'd venture farther if he could
but knew to rest and feared the likelihood

of failure if he tried to cross the fence.
And in his stage of life, he now can sense
that what he used to leap with confidence
could someday soon be cause for consequence

that he would not surmount. And so, he stays
where he is safe and acts content to graze
this edge of grassland. Yet his stance betrays
his thoughts and memories of younger days.

It shows that he can likely now recall
that in his youth, he had the wherewithal
to hold his own with any in a brawl.
Though grayed with age, he still looks broad and tall.

At times, he still can strike a grewsome pose.
He was a young buck once that few'd oppose.
He'd joined in heated fight and slew some foes.
He'd roamed the moonlit night and knew some does.

But now those days are done, and he is old.
Now, when the young bucks meet, he must withhold
his urge to join the game but be consoled
by memories of being strong—and bold.

He does not stand and hold his head up high
with pride for deeds that served to glorify
his status in his herd but seems to sigh
with downcast eyes. His bearing might imply

that though he tried to live with dignity,
he looks back with regret to some degree,
for all he could have been but feared to be,
and all he should have known yet failed to see.

And now, he can't relive the life he's led
nor choose to walk a different path instead.
He can't go back; he must press on ahead
and finish soon this trail he chose to tread.

I raise my gaze and ponder this until
from our front porch, my wife calls up the hill,
"Will you come home soon, dear? You'll catch a chill!"
I wave and answer, "Yes, my sweet, I will."

I like to think, in these experiences we refer to as lifetimes, each of us has something to learn or something to teach.

And no matter how long or brief, every life is complete, adding experience to the collective consciousness that is the living universe.

During the few weeks that I had the privilege of knowing and befriending Gary Feichtinger, I could see that he had learned far more than most. I also feel that he taught me a great deal, for which I am eternally grateful.

The Last Place on Earth

The last place on earth you should have gone
was the U.S. Navy recruiting office.
You could have had your choice of options after
graduating second in your class
from Duke University, in physics.

The only son from an affluent home
in Arlington, Virginia, your father working
in the Pentagon, a GS-15
high-ranking civilian, could have offered
every opportunity you'd wish.

You should at least have been an officer,
But you enlisted as a common seaman.
After boot camp, you were ordered to
return to help with training new recruits.
It was the last place they should have used you.

You showed up driving your Volkswagen van,
white with bright red wording on its side
proclaiming, "And God said:" followed by
Maxwell's mathematical equations
for light. The authorities were in the dark.

They refused to issue your van a base pass,
declaring it was "anti-American."
You tried in vain to explain the physics joke
in your amused, not condescending way,
which only escalated their resolve.

They showed you who was boss, by transferring
you to the last place on Earth that one
would choose to go, the YR-71,
a barge anchored in a tributary
of the Mekong River in Vietnam.

You went there willingly and served with honor,
tried your best to do the wrong thing right,
until you couldn't do it anymore,
as you felt duty bound to disobey,
all illegal or immoral orders.

They sent you to the last place you belonged,
the legal hold for prisoners at Nha Be,
where five times every day you fell in line
with criminals and cowards, then picked up trash
and cigarette butts while awaiting trial.

They should have, rather, set you to the task
of solving world peace, or climate change,
renewable energy or ending hunger.
At least in your case, they permitted you
to walk into the village in the evenings.

There you met a local Buddhist priest
who taught you Zen and Numerology.
You took me there to meet him, though he said
we'd been acquainted in a former life,
and I was still a mystery to him.

On base, when you had free time, you would jog
and wear your black pajamas and straw hat,
looking rather like the Viet Cong.
You'd join me for a workout, then some katas,
and share your plans for after you'd get home.

You planned to start a commune of your own,
on a mountain in America's Southwest.
We'd both read B. F. Skinner's *Walden Two*.
You talked about the possibilities
of building your own place of peace on Earth.

The Navy didn't know what to make of you
when you refused the lawyer they assigned
and said that you would rather speak yourself,
because objecting conscientiously
was strange to them, and they didn't comprehend.

I left you there when I went to the bush
out near Cambodia for several months.
That was the last time I ever saw you.
The next time I was passing through Nha Be,
I asked about you. Someone told me how

you beat their best and won your case; how you
had been sent on to be discharged with honor.
I smiled at the thought of you somewhere,
at last building a better place on earth.
I wondered if I'd ever see you there.

The days and years and decades came and went,
but I would sometimes fondly think of you
and wonder if you found your mountain top,
or got your PhD and started teaching,
maybe doing research for some lab.

Or I supposed you'd be retired by now,
though probably still fit and trim, a vegan
with a charming wife and happy grandkids.
You'd drive a Volvo, live out in the suburbs,
But where? D.C? Denver? San Diego?

Ironically, it was Memorial Day
and forty-nine years since I saw you last,
when I thought to Google search your name.
I found an entry on the World Wide Web,
where you are, and how long you've been there.

For all these years, since only several weeks
after I saw you last, you've been in—
the last place on Earth I should have thought
that I'd find you—back home in Arlington,
Section 6-KK, Row 17, Site 1.

Finding Gary as I did made me think about others with whom I had once served. It occurred to me there was another to whom I owe a debt, a lieutenant junior grade who was my superior officer at my first duty station, while I was still a non-rated seaman, before I left there to go to SERE school and then to Vietnam.

Think of Grace Kelly's face on Marilyn Monroe's body, wrapped in the dress blues of a naval officer . . .

Alice

I don't know why you chose me for a friend,
so far below your rank in every sense.
Was it because you would need no defense
from one so low, I dared not dream – pretend

I could be more? A mere enlisted man,
and you an officer and stunning beauty.
I'd know my place and only do my duty,
follow orders. Before long, we began

to talk of other things and spent some time
together at your place. You prompted me
to read Thoreau. You said that you could see,
in articles I wrote, his paradigm.

You couldn't talk to other men on base.
They all just leered at you then shared their lewd
remarks behind your back. They only viewed
and lusted for your figure and your face.

When I transferred to Vietnam and you
to Pearl Harbor, you still kept in touch
by writing to me often, just as much
as family and friends, though they were few.

You coaxed me to keep writing poetry
and praised the ones I sent you in the mail.
You said it was my task; I should not fail
to witness war, then show society

what I have seen by writing from the heart.
I feared I wasn't worthy of the role,
and it inflicted sickness in my soul,
but I would try and learn to do my part.

You wrote that you had married a Marine,
a major stationed there. And I felt glad
you found someone to trust and finally had
another man whose motives weren't obscene.

Things changed for me. I don't know to this day
just how I came to be a hundred miles
from where I had been last. My letters, files,
your address, and new name were cut away

from me with all the rest. I had to start
again, with what was left. I could not write
to you, so I concluded that you might
not need me anymore; it's well we part.

But I still think of you as an old friend
and wish I had a way to let you know
I am still writing poems, and although
I am unknown and violate the trend

in poetry today, I have no choice
but carry out the task that you assigned.
It is a duty that I owe mankind.
I write the words but hear another's voice.

I chose to close rather than open with the titular piece of this collection. I did this because of its message.

I believe that message is intended for you, the reader, as much as it was for me. By passing it on, I carry out the order given to me and fulfil my mission.

Now, it is for you to do likewise.

While a student at Mansfield University, one of my part-time jobs was working for the English Department as a teaching assistant and tutor, helping with the lower-level English and composition classes. One quiet afternoon, alone in the writing center in an office on the second floor of South Hall, I had a gap between appointments. Grateful for the break, I wearily sat at an empty, wooden desk.

In a few seconds, the desktop faded into a barren plain with sand, stone, sparse vegetation, a rock cliff wall to the left and a surging surf assaulting a beach farther off toward the right.

Straight ahead in the distance, I saw a shimmering mirage which solidified into a dark horse and rider coming hard toward me. As it drew near, I saw it to be a great beast bearing a bearded man clad in ancient Greek armor. He galloped right up to me, reigned back to a broadside stop, looked down at me, and proclaimed the words that follow in the last poem.

When he was done, he turned his horse and began to slowly trot away. As he did so, he dissolved, leaving only that barren plain and then the empty desk in South Hall.

Before his words would also vanish, I pulled a notebook from my backpack and wrote this down:

The Admonition of Ares

You there! Mount your steed and ride
to every country, far and wide.
Tell all the people who abide
there what you saw this day.

Tell them it will soon be night,
and they must cease their futile fight
for neither side can see their plight
when Hatred hides the way.

It's Greed that feeds the drum and fife
and wields the blood-encrusted knife
that tears asunder man from wife
and tramples the child at play.

Hurry! There is little time
to save them. It is not the crime
but the convicted who must climb
the gallows steps and pay.

Warriors fall to their demise
while war survives, in thin disguise,
till Greed and Hatred start to rise
again, and flags display.

You must help them to survive.
If mankind is to stay alive,
all must unite their force and strive
to Greed and Hatred slay.

About the Author

Dave Muffley lives on a remote, wooded slope in the endless mountains of north-central Pennsylvania. He is retired now but has worked as a musician, sailor, soldier, mechanic, race car driver, tech school teacher, park ranger, criminal investigator, chief of police, journalist, and social worker.

Through the provisions of the VA's Disabled Veterans Rehabilitation Program, Dave earned a BA in Mass Communication/Journalism from Mansfield University. Dave believes that, like journalists, poets have a duty to be the watchdogs of society.

Leonard Bernstein, the late, celebrated conductor of the New York Philharmonic Orchestra once stated that music is the language of emotion. Dave extrapolates that art, generally, is the image of emotion, that literature is art's most explicit medium, and poetry is literature's purest art form. Dave's personal definition of art is, that which conveys emotion from the artist to the audience.

Perhaps Dave's most emotionally compelling work is his war poetry. Regarding the poetry of war, Dave suggests that from before the time of Homer, through the Dark Ages to the present dark age, its message has, tragically, still not been overstated.

Although Dave has been writing verse since 1970, he has only recently begun to release his work for publication. *Admonitions of Ares* is his first collection of poems. Its intent and purpose are to convey emotion.

Dave acknowledges that it is intense, but he promises it won't leave a scar.

www.ingramcontent.com/pod-product-compliance
Ingram Content Group UK Ltd.
Pitfield, Milton Keynes, MK11 3LW, UK
UKHW020139250726
13967UKWH00002B/759

9 781716 518836